the F.O.R.E.V.E.R. W.E.D. WORKBOOK for Couples

Building Blocks for a Lasting Love Story

Dr. Cedric D. Alford

@ Copyright 2023 by Dr. Cedric D. Alford, MBA – All rights reserved.

All rights reserved. No part of this publication may be reproduced, distributed, or transmitted in any form or by any means, including photocopying, recording, electronic or mechanical methods, without the prior written permission of the publisher, except in the case of brief quotations embodied in critical reviews and certain other noncommercial uses permitted by copyright law.

This publication is provided "as is", without warranty of any kind, express or implied, including but not limited to the warranties of merchantability, fitness for a particular purpose, or non-infringement.

While Dr. Cedric D. Alford has made every effort to ensure the accuracy and completeness of information contained in this workbook, neither TheDrCed Leadership Development LLC nor the author assumes any responsibility for errors, inaccuracies, omissions, or any inconsistency herein. Any slights of people, places, or organizations are unintentional.

ISBN: Paperback 978-0-9971448-3-3

Published by TheDrCed Leadership Development LLC

Book layout and cover design by Olga Pomazanova
Photo on the cover: unsplash.com

For information regarding permission requests, write to:

Dr. Cedric D. Alford, MBA
TheDrCed Leadership Development LLC
P.O. Box 616, Rowlett, Texas 75048-0616
Email: dralford@thedrced.com

Printed in the United States of America.

Dedication

This book is dedicated to couples at the threshold of their marital journey and those seeking to deepen their bond. Your pursuit of understanding, wisdom, and the aspiration for a stronger, healthier relationship is a testament to the enduring power of love and commitment. May this book serve as a conversation starter, offering perspectives and sparking discussions that enrich your unique path toward marital bliss.

Love recognizes no barriers. It jumps hurdles, leaps fences, penetrates walls to arrive at its destination full of hope.

— *Maya Angelou*

Table of Contents

Dedication	3
PREFACE Introducing the F.O.R.E.V.E.R. W.E.D. Workbook for Couples	7
Acknowledgements	9
PROLOGUE Crafting Your Relationship Biography	11
CHAPTER 1 F: Flexibility	27
CHAPTER 2 O: Open Communication	37
CHAPTER 3 R: Respect	47
CHAPTER 4 E: Empathy	57
CHAPTER 5 V: Vulnerability	67
CHAPTER 6 E: Empowerment	77
CHAPTER 7 R: Resilience	87
CHAPTER 8 W: Wellness	97
CHAPTER 9 E: Emotional Intelligence	107
CHAPTER 10 D: Devotion	117
Final Reflections on F.O.R.E.V.E.R. W.E.D.	127
References	129
About the Author	135

PREFACE

Introducing the F.O.R.E.V.E.R. W.E.D. Workbook for Couples

Welcome to the *F.O.R.E.V.E.R. W.E.D. workbook*, your collaborative journey towards a thriving and enduring marriage. This approach uniquely merges academic insights and Christian values to offer you and your partner a comprehensive blueprint for strengthening your bond. As you delve into the *F.O.R.E.V.E.R. W.E.D.* principles, you will gain invaluable tools to navigate the multifaceted world of marriage.

The *F.O.R.E.V.E.R. W.E.D.* acronym stands for Flexibility, Open communication, Respect, Empathy, Vulnerability, Empowerment, Resilience, Wellness, Emotional Intelligence, and Devotion. These are the foundational pillars of a prosperous marriage. In this workbook, we will dive deep into each principle's academic reasoning and biblical basis, ensuring a balanced perspective that resonates with both the head and heart.

As you progress, you'll be introduced to scholarly and Christian perspectives, deepening your understanding of their importance in a successful marriage. Practical strategies will guide you in integrating these principles into your daily interactions, with each chapter shedding light on their significance using biblical verses and research-driven insights.

Recognizing that every marital journey is unique, the *F.O.R.E.V.E.R. W.E.D.* model is flexible. It encourages you to tailor its principles to fit your relationship's dynamics and needs. This workbook is not a one-size-fits-all guide but rather a resource adaptable to the rhythm of your partnership.

I urge you both to engage with this material with open hearts to deepen your understanding of each other and your shared bond. By embracing the *F.O.R.E.V.E.R. W.E.D.* framework, you'll find yourselves better poised to face challenges and celebrate the beautiful moments of lifelong commitment.

Embark on this transformative journey with passion and a genuine sense of discovery. I sincerely hope that the *F.O.R.E.V.E.R. W.E.D.* principles become the cornerstone of a marriage filled with joy, resilience, and mutual growth.

Warm regards,
Dr. Cedric Alford

Acknowledgements

Crafting this workbook has been one of profound reflection, exploration, and gratitude. The F.O.R.E.V.E.R. W.E.D. model is designed on the tapestry of personal experiences, invaluable lessons learned from couples who have graced my life, and insights gained over years of navigating the intricate dance of marriage. At the heart of this journey is my wife, my compass, my partner in all things, my beloved Bonita. Our shared life, with its joys, trials, triumphs, and lessons, has been the real-world laboratory for the principles outlined in this book.

To the many couples whose paths have crossed ours, friends, neighbors, and acquaintances, each unique way has enriched our understanding of what it means to be in a marriage. We've admired some, learned from others, and sometimes decided to take a different path. Each experience contributed invaluable pieces to this complex puzzle. My faith has been a beacon throughout this journey, guiding my steps and infusing my life and work with purpose and resilience. It has shaped my views and served as the bedrock upon which many principles in this book are built.

My gratitude extends heartfully to our children, our greatest gifts, who have continuously given us reasons to strive, to learn, and to grow better every day. Lex and Tyler, your perspectives and journeys have been enlightening and humbling. You've taught us invaluable lessons and deepened our understanding of ourselves and each other. This book is a guide to a beautiful and enduring marriage. It's not about perfection; it's about growth, understanding, and ceaseless love. Thank you for joining me on this journey, and may you find in these pages the tools, insights, and inspiration to navigate your own F.O.R.E.V.E.R. W.E.D. journey.

PROLOGUE

Crafting Your Relationship Biography

What Shaped Your Love?

Lesson Objective: Encourage couples to delve deep into their life trajectories, culminating in a living autobiography until their paths converge, with the 'Biographical Relationship Explanation™,' serving as a blueprint.

Commencing this workbook requires a foundational step: drafting your living autobiography using the initial blueprint provided by the 'Biographical Relationship Explanation.' This isn't about penning a bestseller or crafting perfect prose; it's akin to providing an editor – your partner – with notes on pivotal experiences, turning points, joys, challenges, and all the nuances that make your life story unique.

Your autobiography is more than just a recount of events. It encapsulates the major heartbeats of your journey – the highs, the lows, the lessons, and the moments that define you. Every section carries weight, from childhood memories to personal challenges and beyond. And while every autobiography will have its shadows, understanding them allows your partner to view your shared perspective with more profound empathy and clarity.

Consider the profound advantage of having read a character's backstory before delving into a novel's main plot. Similarly, by understanding your partner's life story and sharing yours, you offer context – a richer dimension to each conversation, discussion, or challenge you'll navigate in this workbook and life.

Dedicating time to this autobiographical endeavor a few days before your first shared lesson is crucial. It's not about having a complete book but comprehensive notes that guide deeper discussions. This groundwork ensures that your future sessions – those that explore the intricate dance of two lives merging – are informed, empathetic, and profound.

Imagine embarking on this transformative journey with a clear roadmap, the context of each other's autobiographies in hand. Your shared voyage is not just about the present but understanding the past that shaped it. Dive into this exploration, hand in hand, understanding each other's paths and weaving them into the beautiful tapestry of 'us.'

Building the Base: Your Relationship Memoir (Draft)

As you create your autobiographies, exploring the chapters and moments that have made you who you are today is essential. These pages aren't just a recollection of events; they're the fabric of your narratives. Before plunging into the depths of the *F.O.R.E.V.E.R. W.E.D.* model, let's understand the structure and substance of your autobiography:

- **Setting Intentions**
  Start by outlining the preface of your story. Reflect on your shared objectives and aspirations. What is the purpose of this joint exploration? Setting the tone and agenda for your shared journey ensures alignment in the coming pages.

- **Childhood Experiences**
  The early chapters of our lives are often foundational. Traverse through the alleys of your childhood, exploring memories that have shaped your perceptions of love, trust, and commitment. Recognizing these formative moments helps you understand the roots of certain behaviors and expectations in your relationship.

- **Family Dynamics**
  Each family story adds unique color and texture to our autobiographies. Revisit the traditions, communication styles, and familial roles that have played a part in your story. Recognizing these patterns can offer insights into aspects of your shared narrative.

- **Past Relationships**
  Previous chapters of romance, both joyous and painful, have a way of influencing our current storyline. By revisiting and discussing past relationships, you're fostering a culture of openness, appreciating the lessons learned, and understanding their imprints on your current narrative.

- **Personal Values**
  These are the recurring themes in every life story. Engage in a conversation about the core values and beliefs that underpin your perspectives on relationships and marriage. Recognizing both commonalities and differences paves the way for mutual respect and understanding.

- **Shared History**
  While your autobiographies chronicle individual lives, there are pages where your stories have already intertwined. Reflect on the significant moments that have defined your shared journey, from serendipitous meetings to challenges overcome.

View this foundational exploration as the rich backdrop for the future chapters you'll co-author. The insights garnered here will set the stage for the more profound engagements of the *F.O.R.E.V.E.R. W.E.D.* model. It's imperative to be deeply invested in this section, laying a solid foundation for the subsequent sections of this workbook.

SETTING INTENTIONS:

What are your hopes for your relationship/marriage?

What are the critical factors for a successful relationship/marriage?

What do you hope to gain from this exercise?

What was your family like when you were growing up?

Who were the significant people in your life (family, friends, mentors, etc.)?

What were some positive and negative experiences that shaped your understanding of relationships?

How did your family handle conflict?

What were the roles of each family member?

How did your parents' relationship/marriage affect your views on relationships?

What were some of the positive and negative aspects of your past relationships?

What did you learn from those experiences?

How have those experiences influenced your current views on relationships?

What are some of your core values and beliefs about relationships/marriage?

How have these values and beliefs developed over time?

What are some areas where you and your partner may have different values or beliefs about relationships/marriage?

What are some key events that have shaped your relationship/marriage?

How have your past experiences influenced your relationship/marriage?

What are some areas where you and your partner have grown together or struggled together?

Maximizing the F.O.R.E.V.E.R. W.E.D. Experience

As you transition into the core of the *F.O.R.E.V.E.R. W.E.D.* model, it's vital to understand how to make the most of this workbook. This section offers a structured journey into shared aspirations, challenges, history, and dreams. Though each lesson is crafted to fit within an hour, the richness of the conversations you'll unearth may sometimes demand more.

Your Power Hour Breakdown

(**Note:** Consider these times as a helpful scaffold, not a rigid boundary.)

ACTIVITY NAME	TIME
Devotional Commencement	3
Purposeful Pondering	2
Insight Exchange	10
Scripture Insights	10
Bonding Over Devotion	20
Constructive Feedback Circle	10
Gratitude Moment	2
Intimate Intercession	3
	60 Minutes

Strategies to Enrich Your Sessions

1. **Prepare in Advance:**
   Before each session, a quick read-through ensures you dive in clearly and purposefully.

2. **Craft a Conducive Atmosphere:**
   A calm setting with muted phones or subtle background music can significantly enhance focus.

3. **Stay Adaptable:**
   Use the 60-minute structure as a foundation, but let the depth and flow of the conversation determine your pace.

4. **Equip for Reflection:**
   Keep various pens at hand for distinct reflections, further inquiries, or emergent thoughts.

5. **Integrate Past Insights:**
   As you navigate a new topic, link to prior sessions' learnings, enriching your present discussion.

6. **Champion Open Dialogue:**
   After each section, converse transparently, ensuring mutual respect and understanding.

7. **Journal Authentically:**
   Documenting your journey isn't about polished notes but raw, genuine revelations.

8. **The Value of the Tangible:**
   A physical workbook can amplify the intimacy of this process. Writing, exchanging thoughts, and tactile engagement can be uniquely bonding.

9. **Anticipate and Prepare:**
   Peek into the next chapter before the session, streamlining your discussion.

Let's journey together! With this book as your guide and your partner by your side, every page turned is a new step toward deepening your bond. Remember, it's about the destination and the beautiful moments you'll share. So, with your hearts in sync and goals in sight, take a deep breath and dive into this dance of discovery. Cheers to a relationship filled with understanding and warmth!

Embarking on Your Journey Together

With the roadmap and the foundations set, it's time to dive deep and explore. This journey will illuminate the nuances of your relationship and foster an environment of growth, understanding, and deeper connection. Together, you'll traverse memories, reflect on shared moments, and chart a course filled with love and understanding for the future.

Grab your partner's hand, set your intentions, and let's embark on this transformative voyage.

Let's dive in!

CHAPTER 1

F: Flexibility

Embracing Adaptability: The Art of Flexibility in Marriage

Lesson Objective: To help you understand the importance of flexibility in marriage and develop skills to adapt and compromise while being inclusive of other religious beliefs.

An Academic Perspective

As explored in academic research, flexibility within marriages reveals its crucial role in nurturing enduring and healthy partnerships. Beyond being a mere trait, flexibility permeates various dimensions of a couple's shared life, significantly contributing to their ability to adapt and flourish amid life's trials.

Research consistently associates flexibility with key indicators of a thriving marriage: marital satisfaction and adjustment. For instance, South, Krueger, and

Iacono (2011) established a strong link between flexibility and heightened marital satisfaction and adjustment levels. Their study underscores adaptability and a willingness to compromise, integral aspects of flexibility, empowering couples to navigate challenges and fostering harmonious relationships effectively.

A significant area where flexibility showcases its importance is communication within marriages. Weger Jr, Castle, and Emmett (2010) validate that flexible communication styles – characterized by empathy, active listening, and a readiness to compromise – correlate with increased marital satisfaction and reduced relationship distress. This implies that couples embracing adaptability in their communication can adeptly manage conflicts and enhance the overall quality of their relationship.

Flexibility also plays a pivotal role in problem-solving and decision-making within marriages. Findings by Randall and Bodenmann (2009) suggest that couples who exhibit greater flexibility in these domains often experience lower levels of relationship distress and heightened satisfaction. Adapting to changing circumstances and considering diverse viewpoints fosters a balanced and resilient marital dynamic.

Maintaining intimacy and emotional connection in marriages equally demands flexibility. A study by Rehman, Rellini, and Fallis (2011) unveiled that flexible expressions of love and affection often increase emotional closeness, enhancing marital satisfaction. Flexibility enables couples to embrace new experiences and accommodate each other's needs, cementing the emotional bond that forms the bedrock of their marital relationship.

As contemporary society redefines gender roles and expectations, flexibility's impact on marriages becomes even more pertinent. Research by Kornrich, Brines, and Leupp (2013) links flexibility in adapting to evolving gender roles to heightened relationship satisfaction. As couples navigate the evolving dynamics of modern relationships, flexibility empowers them to forge a balanced, supportive, and fulfilling partnership.

For instance, consider a couple confronting a significant life change, such as a job offer requiring relocation. Couples embodying flexibility can openly discuss their concerns, evaluate the potential impacts on their relationship, and deliberate on the decision's pros and cons. Their willingness to compromise and adapt to new situations allows them to navigate changes unitedly, reinforcing their bond and maintaining the quality of their relationship.

Prioritizing flexibility across their interactions, be it in communication, problem-solving, decision-making, expressing affection, or adapting to changing gender roles, tends to guide couples toward increased marital satisfaction, enhanced adjustment, and greater resilience against challenges. Therefore, nurturing flexibility offers a robust mechanism for couples in diverse life stages to navigate their shared journey successfully.

Biblical Foundation

Ephesians 4:2 (NIV) – "Be completely humble and gentle; be patient, bearing with one another in love."

Philippians 2:4 (NIV) – "Let each of you look not only to his own interests but also to the interests of others."

Explanation

In nurturing a healthy marriage, fostering flexibility emerges as a crucial quality. This entails adapting to changing circumstances and collaborating with your partner to discover solutions that benefit both. But how do these biblical verses align with the concept of flexibility in marriage?

Let's commence with Ephesians 4:2. This verse urges us to approach our partners with humility, gentleness, and patience. It reminds us that differences in perspective are natural, and it's okay. At times, flexibility and compromise are necessary to fortify our marriage. We can surmount challenges and obstacles by embracing each other with love.

Next, consider Philippians 2:4. This verse encourages us not to solely focus on our concerns but also consider our partner's interests. Flexibility enables us to step into our partner's shoes, understanding their viewpoint. It empowers us to collaborate on solutions that benefit both rather than solely prioritizing our preferences.

So, what do these verses signify for you as a couple aspiring to cultivate flexibility in your marriage? They underscore the significance of patience, kindness, and the readiness to collaborate for mutually beneficial solutions. By practicing humility and placing your partner's needs at the forefront, you can establish a robust and adaptable marriage capable of weathering any challenges.

Summary

Flexibility emerges as a cornerstone in the realm of lasting and fulfilling marriages. Rooted deeply in academic research, flexibility is a multifaceted trait, encompassing adaptability in communication, problem-solving, decision-making, and the ability to adjust to evolving societal dynamics. Equally, biblical teachings emphasize humility, patience, and mutual respect, aligning seamlessly with the tenets of flexibility. The confluence of both these academic findings and spiritual teachings suggests that couples who foster flexibility can not only navigate the complexities of modern relationships but also enrich their marital bond.

Couples must embrace flexibility, understanding, and the art of mutual compromise to thrive in marriage's ever-evolving landscape.

Applying The Lesson: Flexibility Power Hour

Activity 1: Devotional Commencement – Flexibility (3 Minutes)
- Together, find a spot and offer a prayer of gratitude for exploring "Flexibility."

Activity 2: Purposeful Pondering (2 Minutes)
- Pause to set joint intentions and share aspirations for the session.

Activity 3: Insight Exchange (10 Minutes)
- Spend 10 minutes writing or reviewing "Flexibility" notes, then share summaries.

Activity 4: Scripture Insights (10 Minutes)
- Read Ephesians 4:2 and Philippians 2:4, discussing insights and applications regarding relationship flexibility. Now, each of you find a different bible verse that speaks to the topic. Discuss your choice and why.

Activity 5: Bonding over Devotion (20 Minutes)

Engage in one activity option either reflecting on past flexibility moments or discussing core relationship values.

- **OPTION A:** Past Reflections – Reflect together on an instance when one demonstrated flexibility and discuss its significance.
- **OPTION B:** Values Visualization – Write down three core values defining your relationship, then share and discuss them.

Activity 6: Constructive Feedback Circle (10 Minutes)
- Reflect on a time flexibility was challenging and discuss how it could have been better.

Activity 7: Gratitude Moment (2 Minutes)
- Share something you're each thankful for about the other.

Activity 8: Intimate Intercession (3 Minutes)

Spend a few minutes in silent meditation and prayer, focusing on each other, and conclude with a joint "Amen."

Lesson Notes and Summary for Sharing

REFLECTIONS

Lesson Notes:

Summary:

Weekly Journal Notes

(Complete before Next Session)

FLEXIBILITY NOTES AND JOURNAL

I WILL:

Continue to:

Stop:

F: Flexibility

I WILL:

Start:

Reflections:

CHAPTER 2

O: Open Communication

The Power of Honesty:
Mastering Open Communication in Your Relationship

Lesson Objective: To help you understand the importance of open communication in marriage and develop skills to express feelings, concerns, and needs effectively.

An Academic Perspective

Open communication is a cornerstone within marriages, deeply explored within academia for its pivotal role in establishing lasting and thriving unions. Venturing beyond mere conversation, open communication reveals multi-faceted layers that extend across various dimensions of marital life.

When it comes to marital satisfaction, the impact of open communication can be substantial. Numerous studies link the quality of communication between partners to marital satisfaction *(Hahlweg, Kaiser, Christensen, Fehm-Wolfsdorf, & Groth, 2000)*. Marked by honesty, transparency, and active listening, open communication is associated with elevated marital contentment. Couples who nurture open communication find themselves better equipped to handle challenges and sustain a strong emotional bond, enriching their relationship journey.

Open communication is vital in conflict resolution and an indispensable element of marital success. Research emphasizes that open communication is pivotal in conflict resolution and reducing relationship distress *(Heavey, Layne, & Christensen, 1993)*. Couples who openly and respectfully express their feelings, needs, and concerns are more likely to discover resolutions that satisfy both parties, nurturing harmony and resilience in their relationship.

Trust and emotional intimacy, the bedrock of any close bond, also experience significant influence from open communication. Studies suggest that couples who engage in open communication tend to feel more secure and emotionally connected *(Laurenceau, Barrett, & Pietromonaco, 1998)*. This heightened emotional closeness not only amplifies marital satisfaction but also acts as a safeguard against relationship dissolution.

The dimension of sexual relationships within marriage also reaps substantial benefits from open communication. Research indicates that couples who engage in candid discussions about their sexual needs and desires report greater sexual and overall relationship satisfaction *(MacNeil & Byers, 2005)*. This openness in addressing an intimate aspect of their relationship fortifies the emotional and physical bond between partners.

Life's inevitable changes pose challenges to marriages, and open communication emerges as invaluable in navigating them. Research illustrates that couples who effectively communicate about life transitions – such as job changes, childbirth, and aging challenges – are better equipped to maintain relationship satisfaction *(Birditt, Wan, Orbuch, & Antonucci, 2017)*. Open communication empowers couples to support each other and navigate life's twists collaboratively, fostering resilience and a lasting partnership.

Imagine a couple in disagreement over allocating financial resources. Open communication enables them to articulate their concerns, needs, and priorities while actively listening to each other. This aids in comprehending each other's viewpoints, identifying potential compromises, and reaching decisions that satisfy both, contributing to the stability and harmony of their relationship.

Couples who prioritize open communication across diverse facets of their marital life – daily interactions, conflict resolution, expressions of intimacy, and life transitions – frequently encounter heightened marital satisfaction, a more profound emotional connection, and enhanced resilience against challenges. Cultivating open communication forms a robust foundation for a successful and gratifying marriage through various stages of life.

Biblical Foundation

James 1:19 (NIV) – "My dear brothers and sisters, take note of this: Everyone should be quick to listen, slow to speak, and slow to become angry."

Proverbs 15:1 (NIV) – "A gentle answer turns away wrath, but a harsh word stirs up anger."

Explanation

Promoting a healthy marriage hinges on open communication – a cornerstone that fosters trust, deepens connections, and helps us overcome challenges. But how do these biblical verses align with open communication in marriage?

Let's begin with James 1:19. This verse encourages us to be swift to listen, slow to speak, and slow to anger. During conversations with our partners, we're called to truly hear their words. It means refraining from interruption or defensiveness and striving to grasp their viewpoint. Doing so lays the groundwork for mutual respect and trust, enabling more open and effective communication.

Now, consider Proverbs 15:1. This verse underscores the power of a gentle response in diffusing anger, while harsh words can escalate tensions. Using kind and gentle words and tones is crucial when communicating with our partner. Even amid frustration or upset, responding with aggression only exacerbates matters. Responding with gentleness and empathy keeps conversations productive and focused on finding solutions.

So, what do these verses signify for you as a couple aspiring to foster open communication in your marriage? They highlight the significance of patience, respect, and kindness in your dialogues. By actively listening and responding gently, you create an environment of safety and support where open communication can flourish.

Summary

Open communication is fundamental in shaping enduring and healthy marriages, as evidenced by academic findings and biblical teachings. Such communication transcends mere conversation and delves into honest expression, active listening, and mutual understanding. Marital satisfaction, conflict resolution, trust, emotional intimacy, and even sexual satisfaction are all notably enhanced by open communication practices. Communicating openly is pivotal when navigating life's inevitable transitions.

From the biblical viewpoint, James 1:19 and Proverbs 15:1 emphasize patience, active listening, and gentle response, reinforcing the essence of effective communication. Together, these teachings and findings underscore the profound impact of open communication, illuminating its role as the heartbeat of a thriving marriage.

By adopting these principles and fostering an environment of trust, understanding, and empathy, couples can pave the way for a marriage marked by profound connection and resilience.

Applying The Lesson
Open Communication Power Hour

Activity 1: Devotional Commencement – Open Communication (3 Minutes)
- Together, find a spot and offer a prayer of gratitude for exploring "Open Communication".

Activity 2: Purposeful Pondering (2 Minutes)
- Pause to set joint intentions and share aspirations for the session.

Activity 3: Insight Exchange (10 Minutes)
- Spend 10 minutes writing or reviewing "Open Communication" notes, then share summaries.

Activity 4: Scripture Insights (10 Minutes)
- Read James 1:19 and Proverbs 15:1 together, taking turns to share insights and personal applications. Now, each of you find a different bible verse that speaks to the topic. Discuss your choice and why.

Activity 5: Bonding over Devotion (20 Minutes)

Choose and immerse yourselves in ONE of the provided activity options, aiming to deepen understanding, enjoy the process, and fortify your connection.

- **OPTION A:** Two Truths and a Desire – Share two honest thoughts and one desire for the relationship. Discuss and provide feedback.
- **OPTION B:** Open Mic – Each partner speaks uninterrupted for 5 minutes about something significant, then discuss.

Activity 6: Constructive Feedback Circle (10 Minutes)
- Reflect on a time open communication was challenging and discuss how it could have been better.

Activity 7: Gratitude Moment (2 Minutes)
- Share something you're each thankful for about the other.

Activity 8: Intimate Intercession (3 Minutes)

Spend a few minutes in silent meditation and prayer, focusing on each other, and conclude with a joint "Amen."

Lesson Notes and Summary for Sharing

REFLECTIONS

Lesson Notes:

Summary:

Weekly Journal Notes

(Complete before Next Session)

FOSTERING COMMUNICATION NOTES AND JOURNAL

I WILL:

Continue to:

Stop:

O: Open Communication

I WILL:

Start:

Reflections:

CHAPTER 3

R: Respect

Respecting One Another: The Key To A Harmonious Marriage

Lesson Objective: To help you understand the importance of mutual respect in marriage and develop skills to honor each other's individuality, thoughts, and feelings.

An Academic Perspective

In marriages, respect has been identified as a critical ingredient that breathes life into a successful and enduring bond. Volumes of academic research explore respect in marriage, casting light on its role in creating an environment that's harmonious and fulfilling for couples across diverse age groups.

Regarding marital satisfaction, the degree of respect that partners hold for one another casts a profound influence. Multiple studies underscore the correlation between mutual respect, which involves acknowledging each other's individuality, thoughts, and feelings, and enhanced levels of marital satisfaction *(Pulerwitz,*

Amaro, De Jong, Gortmaker, & Rudd, 2002). Couples displaying respect towards each other stand a better chance at preserving a strong emotional connection and deftly navigating relationship challenges, thereby creating a more fulfilling relationship milieu.

Respect also carries significant weight in resolving conflicts, a critical aspect that shapes the stability and success of any marriage. Numerous studies suggest that communication imbued with respect during conflicts fosters constructive resolutions and decreases relationship distress *(Gottman, 1994)*. When disagreements are navigated respectfully, couples are more likely to find mutually satisfying solutions, thereby nurturing harmony and resilience within their relationship.

Trust and emotional intimacy between partners are also shaped mainly by respect. Research findings indicate that couples extending mutual respect tend to experience higher security and emotional connectedness in their relationship *(Gottman, 1994)*. This emotional closeness not only amplifies marital satisfaction but also acts as a bulwark against the potential dissolution of the relationship.

The maintenance of a healthy sexual relationship within marriage is another area where respect proves to be vital. Studies point out that couples demonstrating respect for each other's boundaries, needs, and desires in their sexual relationship enjoy greater sexual satisfaction and overall relationship satisfaction *(MacNeil & Byers, 2005)*. By fostering respect in this intimate realm of their relationship, couples can enhance their emotional and physical bond.

Respect also significantly influences how couples manage the unavoidable changes that life presents. Research indicates that couples demonstrating respect for each other's opinions, feelings, and needs during life transitions, such as job changes, the birth of a child, or the challenges of aging, are more adept at maintaining their relationship satisfaction *(Birditt, Wan, Orbuch, & Antonucci, 2017)*. Respect equips couples with the ability to support one another and journey through these changes together, fostering a resilient and enduring partnership.

Consider a situation where a couple has different opinions regarding parenting styles. Suppose they approach this situation with mutual respect. In that case, they can effectively listen to each other's perspectives, acknowledge the validity of each other's opinions, and collaboratively develop a parenting approach that respects both partners' values and preferences. This process, underscored by respect, not only preserves the harmony and stability of their relationship but also effectively addresses the issue at hand.

Couples who infuse respect into their interactions, conflict resolution strategies, expressions of intimacy, and approach to life transitions tend to experience greater marital satisfaction, more robust emotional connections, and increased resilience when dealing with challenges. Cultivating respect in their relationship paves the way for couples to construct a successful and rewarding marriage regardless of age.

Biblical Foundation

1 Peter 3:7 (NIV) – "In the same way, you husbands must give honor to your wives. Treat your wife with understanding as you live together. She may be weaker than you are, but she is your equal partner in God's gift of new life. Treat her as you should, so your prayers will not be hindered."

Ephesians 4:32 (NIV) – "Be kind and compassionate to one another, forgiving each other, just as in Christ God forgave you."

Explanation

Respect is a crucial component of any healthy marriage. When we treat our partner with honor, kindness, and understanding, we create an environment of mutual respect and support that allows our relationship to thrive. So, how do these biblical verses tie into respect in marriage?

Let's start with 1 Peter 3:7. This verse speaks explicitly to husbands, reminding them to honor their wives and treat them with understanding. It emphasizes that while wives may be physically weaker, they are equal partners in God's gift of new life. Treating our wives with the respect they deserve can create a foundation of mutual trust and support that allows our marriage to flourish. The verse notes that treating our wives with respect is essential for our spiritual well-being, as our prayers may be hindered if we fail.

In Ephesians 4:32, this verse encourages us to be kind, compassionate, and forgiving towards each other. It reminds us that we should forgive each other just as God has forgiven us. When we let go of anger and resentment and approach each other with kindness and compassion, we create an environment of respect and understanding that strengthens our marriage.

So, what do these verses mean for you as a couple who wants to cultivate respect in your marriage? They emphasize the importance of treating each other with honor, understanding, kindness, and forgiveness. Practicing respect in daily interactions can create a safe and supportive environment where both partners feel valued and heard.

Summary

Mutual respect is a pivotal component in solidifying a lasting and harmonious marriage. Academically speaking, respect is closely associated with marital satisfaction, constructive conflict resolution, trust, emotional intimacy, sexual satisfaction, and the ability to adapt to life's inevitable changes. Demonstrating respect towards one's partner means recognizing and honoring their individuality, emotions, thoughts, and boundaries. This essence of respect is echoed in biblical verses. 1 Peter 3:7 emphasizes the importance of husbands honoring their wives, treating them as equals, and recognizing their significance in the marital bond. Ephesians 4:32 advises kindness, compassion, and forgiveness, fostering an environment where respect thrives. .

For couples aspiring to maintain a deeply connected and harmonious union, mutual respect is a cornerstone, enhancing their relationship and spiritual well-being. When woven with biblical principles and cultural insights, respect transforms into a guiding force, enriching every facet of marital life.

Applying The Lesson: Respect Power Hour

Activity 1: Devotional Commencement – Mutual Respect (3 Minutes)
- Together, find a spot and offer a prayer of gratitude for exploring "Mutual Respect"

Activity 2: Purposeful Pondering (2 Minutes)
- Pause to set joint intentions and share aspirations for the session.

Activity 3: Insight Exchange (10 Minutes)
- Spend 10 minutes writing or reviewing "Mutual Respect" notes, then share summaries.

Activity 4: Scripture Insights (10 Minutes)
- Read 1 Peter 3:7 and Ephesians 4:32 together, taking turns to share insights and personal applications. Now, each of you find a different bible verse that speaks to the topic. Discuss your choice and why.

Activity 5: Bonding over Devotion (20 Minutes)
Choose and immerse yourselves in ONE of the provided activity options, aiming to deepen understanding, enjoy the process, and fortify your connection.

- **OPTION A:** Respectful Recollection – Share a time when the other showed immense respect, and discuss its impact.
- **OPTION B:** Respectful Response Game – Take turns sharing a definition of respect. The other responds respectfully, and both discuss the experience.

Activity 6: Constructive Feedback Circle (10 Minutes)
- Reflect on a time mutual respect was challenging and discuss how it could have been better.

Activity 7: Gratitude Moment (2 Minutes)
- Share something you're each thankful for about the other.

Activity 8: Intimate Intercession (3 Minutes)
Spend a few minutes in silent meditation and prayer, focusing on each other, and conclude with a joint "Amen."

R: Respect

Lesson Notes and Summary for Sharing

REFLECTIONS

Lesson Notes:

Summary:

Weekly Journal Notes

(Complete before Next Session)

RESPECT NOTES AND JOURNAL

I WILL:

Continue to:

Stop:

R: Respect

I WILL:

Start:

Reflections:

CHAPTER 4

E: Empathy

The Empathy Connection: Deepening Your Emotional Bond

Lesson Objective: To help you understand the importance of empathy in marriage and develop skills to understand and share each other's feelings while being inclusive of other religious beliefs.

An Academic Perspective

Empathy is a cornerstone of successful marriages, serving as a critical catalyst for enduring and robust bonds. Academic research extensively explores empathy's role within the marriage framework, shedding light on its influence in fostering a nurturing environment for couples at varying life stages.

The empathy quotient between partners significantly impacts marital satisfaction. A body of research highlights a strong correlation between mutual empathy – understanding and sharing each other's feelings, perspectives, and experiences – and elevated levels of marital satisfaction *(Long et al., 1999)*. Empathy enables couples to sustain a robust emotional connection and skillfully navigate relationship hurdles, creating a more rewarding relationship atmosphere.

Conflict resolution, integral to marital stability and prosperity, is markedly influenced by empathic communication. Studies indicate that empathetic discourse during disagreements leads to more productive outcomes and mitigates relationship distress *(Segrin et al., 2007)*. An empathetic approach to conflicts guides couples toward mutually satisfying solutions, fostering an atmosphere of harmony and resilience.

Empathy shared between partners profoundly impacts establishing and maintaining trust and emotional intimacy. Evidence suggests that couples demonstrating consistent empathy experience a more profound sense of security and emotional connectedness *(Cramer, 2004)*. This bond of emotional intimacy augments marital satisfaction and fortifies the relationship against potential disruptions.

Empathy also plays a pivotal role in maintaining a healthy sexual relationship within marriage. Research shows that couples who display empathy for each other's desires, needs, and boundaries in their sexual relationship enjoy a higher degree of sexual and overall relationship satisfaction *(Byers, 2005)*. Fostering empathy within this intimate dimension enhances partners' emotional and physical bond.

Empathy's significance extends to managing life's inevitable changes and transitions. Research confirms that couples who demonstrate empathy for each other's feelings, opinions, and needs during transitions – job changes, parenthood, aging – retain their relationship satisfaction more effectively *(Pietromonaco et al., 2013)*. Empathy equips couples to offer mutual support and weather these life transitions cohesively, nurturing a resilient and lasting partnership.

In practice, imagine a couple disagreeing on financial management. Approaching the issue empathetically allows a better understanding of each other's perspectives, validates the other's feelings, and collaborates on a financial plan that respects both partners' concerns and preferences. This empathetic method ensures relationship harmony and stability while addressing the matter.

Moreover, studies on empathetic distress in couples facing chronic illness reveal that partners who exhibit empathy towards ailing partners foster better coping mechanisms and psychological adaptation, reinforcing the relationship's emotional strength *(Langer et al., 2009)*.

By weaving empathy into interactions, conflict resolutions, intimate expressions, and life transitions, couples can experience enriched marital satisfaction, fortified emotional bonds, and heightened resilience against challenges. Cultivating empathy in their relationship lays the foundation for a successful and rewarding marriage that transcends age barriers.

Biblical Foundation

Romans 12:15 (NIV) – "Rejoice with those who rejoice; mourn with those who mourn."

Explanation

Galatians 6:2 (NIV) – "Carry each other's burdens, and in this way you will fulfill the law of Christ."

Empathy is a crucial element of a healthy marriage. When we can put ourselves in our partner's shoes and truly understand their thoughts and feelings, we can build a deeper connection and a more fulfilling relationship. So, how do these biblical verses tie into the idea of empathy in marriage?

Let's start with Romans 12:15. This verse reminds us to rejoice with those who rejoice and mourn with those who mourn. In other words, we should be sensitive to our partner's emotional state and willing to share their joys and sorrows. When we empathize with our partner this way, we create a more profound sense of intimacy and understanding that allows our marriage to thrive.

Galatians 6:2, this verse encourages us to carry each other's burdens. When we're willing to help our partners through difficult times and share in their struggles, we create a bond of mutual support and understanding that can help us weather any storm. By fulfilling the law of Christ in this way, we not only strengthen our relationship with our partner but also our relationship with God.

So, what do these verses mean for you as a couple who wants to cultivate empathy in your marriage? They emphasize the importance of being sensitive to each other's emotions and willing to share their joys and struggles. Practicing empathy in your daily interactions can create a more intimate and fulfilling relationship built on mutual understanding and support.

Summary

Empathy stands as a vital pillar for fostering lasting and profound marital connections. From an academic standpoint, empathy correlates with heightened marital satisfaction, constructive conflict resolution, trust, and emotional intimacy. The practice of empathy in relationships aids couples in effectively navigating life's transitions and challenges, from managing finances to supporting partners in times of illness. As illustrated in Romans 12:15 and Galatians 6:2, the Bible's teachings echo the significance of empathetic connections, urging individuals to share their partners' joys and burdens. This mutual understanding nurtures the marital bond and deepens one's spiritual connection with God.

For couples looking to enrich their marital lives, empathy becomes instrumental. It offers a pathway to understanding, trust, and emotional bonding, strengthened further by biblical insights and an inclusive approach to diverse cultural and religious perspectives.

Applying The Lesson: Empathy Power Hour

Activity 1: Devotional Commencement – Empathy (3 Minutes)
- Together, find a spot and offer a prayer of gratitude for exploring "Empathy".

Activity 2: Purposeful Pondering (2 Minutes)
- Pause to set joint intentions and share aspirations for the session.

Activity 3: Insight Exchange (10 Minutes)
- Spend 10 minutes writing or reviewing "Empathy" notes, then share summaries.

Activity 4: Scripture Insights (10 Minutes)
- Read Romans 12:15 and Galatians 6:2 together, taking turns to share insights and personal applications. Now, each of you find a different bible verse that speaks to the topic. Discuss your choice and why.

Activity 5: Bonding over Devotion (20 Minutes)
Choose and immerse yourselves in ONE of the provided activity options, aiming to deepen understanding, enjoy the process, and fortify your connection.

- **OPTION A:** Empathy Shoes – Share a recent feeling or challenge. The other tries to express understanding, then discuss.
- **OPTION B:** Empathy Cards – Write down a current emotional state or challenge, swap, and discuss ways to support each other.

Activity 6: Constructive Feedback Circle (10 Minutes)
- Reflect on a time empathy was challenging and discuss how it could have been better.

Activity 7: Gratitude Moment (2 Minutes)
- Share something you're each thankful for about the other.

Activity 8: Intimate Intercession (3 Minutes)
Spend a few minutes in silent meditation and prayer, focusing on each other, and conclude with a joint "Amen."

Lesson Notes and Summary for Sharing

REFLECTIONS

Lesson Notes:

Summary:

Weekly Journal Notes

(Complete before Next Session)

EMPATHY NOTES AND JOURNAL

I WILL:

Continue to:

Stop:

I WILL:

Start:

Reflections:

CHAPTER 5

V: Vulnerability

Revealing Your True Self:
The Importance Of Vulnerability In Marriage

Lesson Objective: To help you understand the importance of vulnerability in marriage and develop skills to be open and authentic with your partner.

An Academic Perspective

Vulnerability, characterized by the courage to be open and authentic with one's partner, is pivotal in maintaining thriving marriages. Academic research highlights the significance of vulnerability in matrimonial bonds, offering relevant insights for couples across different stages of life.

A profusion of studies reveals that marital satisfaction is intrinsically tied to the degree of vulnerability shared between partners. Couples who choose to be vulnerable by transparently expressing their innermost thoughts and feelings are better equipped to foster a robust emotional connection and navigate relational hurdles, thereby cultivating more fulfilling relationships *(Reis & Shaver, 1988)*. This positive correlation between vulnerability and marital satisfaction underlines the importance of creating safe spaces for open communication within the relationship.

Conflict resolution, a linchpin for the longevity and health of a marriage, also greatly benefits from the practice of vulnerability. Empirical evidence suggests that engaging in vulnerable communication during disputes often results in more productive solutions and reduces relationship distress *(Siffert & Schwarz, 2011)*. By navigating disagreements with vulnerability, couples enhance their chances of achieving mutually satisfying resolutions, nurturing harmony and resilience.

Vulnerability is also instrumental in fostering trust and emotional intimacy between partners. Studies indicate that when couples demonstrate vulnerability, they are more likely to feel secure and emotionally bonded in their relationship *(Mikulincer & Shaver, 2007)*. This emotional closeness heightens marital satisfaction and is a buffer against potential relationship breakdowns.

The importance of vulnerability also extends to the sexual dimension of marriage. Research reveals that couples who openly discuss their sexual desires, fears, and boundaries tend to experience higher sexual and overall relationship satisfaction *(MacNeil & Byers, 2005)*. Couples can deepen their emotional connection and physical intimacy through vulnerability in their intimate interactions.

Vulnerability also plays a significant role in navigating the inevitable changes and transitions that punctuate the course of a marriage. Research indicates that when couples approach significant life transitions, such as career changes, childbirth, or the challenges of aging, with vulnerability, they can better adapt and sustain their relationship satisfaction *(Birditt, Wan, Orbuch, & Antonucci, 2017)*. This openness allows couples to lean on each other during challenging times, fostering resilience and the longevity of the partnership.

For instance, in a scenario where one partner grapples with a severe illness, the power of vulnerability becomes evident. Through open and authentic communication, both partners can share their fears and emotions, offering each other understanding and support. Such communication alleviates the stress and anxiety related to the illness while preserving the relationship's harmony and stability amidst adversity.

Couples who infuse vulnerability into their interactions, conflict resolution, expressions of intimacy, and transitions will likely reap the rewards of increased marital satisfaction, stronger emotional connections, and heightened resilience.

Explanation

Vulnerability is a crucial aspect of building a healthy and fulfilling marriage. When we can be open and honest with our partner about our thoughts, feelings, and struggles, we create a more profound sense of intimacy and trust that allows our relationship to thrive. So, how do these biblical verses tie into the idea of vulnerability in marriage?

Biblical Foundation

2 Corinthians 12:9 (NIV) – "But he said to me, 'My grace is sufficient for you, for my power is made perfect in weakness.' Therefore I will boast all the more gladly about my weaknesses so that Christ's power may rest on me."

James 5:16 (NIV) – "Therefore confess your sins to each other and pray for each other so that you may be healed. The prayer of a righteous person is powerful and effective."

Let's start with 2 Corinthians 12:9. This verse reminds us that God's power is made perfect in weakness. In other words, when we're vulnerable and honest about our weaknesses and struggles, we allow God's power to work through us. Being open and honest with our partner about our vulnerabilities can create a more profound sense of trust and intimacy that strengthens our marriage.

In James 5:16, this verse encourages us to confess our sins and pray for each other. When we're willing to be vulnerable about our mistakes and shortcomings, we create an environment of honesty and forgiveness that allows our relationship to flourish. We build a stronger and more resilient marriage by praying for each other and supporting each other through difficult times.

So, what do these verses mean for you as a couple who wants to cultivate vulnerability in your marriage? They emphasize the importance of being open and honest with each other about your weaknesses, struggles, and mistakes. Practicing vulnerability in your daily interactions can create a more profound sense of intimacy and trust, allowing your marriage to thrive.

Summary

Vulnerability is essential for cultivating and sustaining deep marital bonds. From an academic viewpoint, vulnerability is closely tied to marital satisfaction, highlighting the value of open communication, conflict resolution, trust, emotional intimacy, and the ability to traverse life's transitions. Couples who are transparent with each other, sharing their deepest thoughts and fears, are better positioned to build strong emotional connections and tackle relationship challenges. Additionally, vulnerability aids in fostering mutual trust, navigating disputes, enhancing intimacy, and bolstering resilience during significant life changes.

The Bible underscores the merits of vulnerability through verses such as 2 Corinthians 12:9 and James 5:16, emphasizing the strength found in acknowledging weakness and the healing power of confession. In marriage, such biblical teachings inspire couples to embrace their vulnerabilities, fostering trust, intimacy, and resilience.

To fully experience the benefits of a fulfilling marriage, couples must practice vulnerability, grounded in academic insights and enriched by biblical wisdom. This approach and respect for diverse religious and cultural perspectives set the stage for a profoundly connected and trusting marital relationship.

Applying The Lesson: Vulnerability Power Hour

Activity 1: Devotional Commencement – Vulnerability (3 Minutes)
- Together, find a spot and offer a prayer of gratitude for exploring "Vulnerability".

Activity 2: Purposeful Pondering (2 Minutes)
- Pause to set joint intentions and share aspirations for the session.

Activity 3: Insight Exchange (10 Minutes)
- Spend 10 minutes writing or reviewing "Vulnerability" notes, then share summaries.

Activity 4: Scripture Insights (10 Minutes)
- Read 2 Corinthians 12:9 and James 5:16 together, taking turns to share insights and personal applications. Now, each of you find a different bible verse that speaks to the topic. Discuss your choice and why.

Activity 5: Bonding over Devotion (20 Minutes)
Choose and immerse yourselves in ONE of the provided activity options, aiming to deepen understanding, enjoy the process, and fortify your connection.

- **OPTION A:** Vulnerable Moment Share – Speak about a recent time you felt vulnerable. Discuss and offer support.
- **OPTION B:** Trust Fall Chat – While it's a physical exercise, after doing a 'trust fall', discuss feelings of vulnerability and trust.

Activity 6: Constructive Feedback Circle (10 Minutes)
- Reflect on a time vulnerability was challenging and discuss how it could have been better.

Activity 7: Gratitude Moment (2 Minutes)
- Share something you're each thankful for about the other.

Activity 8: Intimate Intercession (3 Minutes)
Spend a few minutes in silent meditation and prayer, focusing on each other, and conclude with a joint "Amen."

Lesson Notes and Summary for Sharing

REFLECTIONS

Lesson Notes:

Summary:

Weekly Journal Notes

(Complete before Next Session)

VULNERABILITY NOTES AND JOURNAL

I WILL:

Continue to:

Stop:

V: Vulnerability

I WILL:

Start:

Reflections:

CHAPTER 6

E: Empowerment

Empowering Each Other: Unleashing Your Partner's Potential

Lesson Objective: To help you understand the importance of empowerment in marriage and develop skills to support each other's personal and professional growth.

An Academic Perspective

*E*mpowerment, a construct highlighting support for personal and professional growth within a relationship, is crucial to thriving marriages. Abundant academic research underscores the significance of empowerment in marital bonds, yielding insights relevant to couples at different stages of their lives.

There is a notable link between marital satisfaction and the degree of empowerment manifested between partners, as underlined by numerous studies. Empowerment, characterized by active support for each other's growth, is positively associated with elevated levels of marital satisfaction *(Rusbult & Van Lange, 2003)*. By empowering each other, couples are better positioned to foster a robust emotional bond and tackle relationship challenges effectively, paving the way for a more gratifying union.

Empowerment is also pivotal in conflict resolution, a key determinant of marriage stability and success. Studies illustrate that empowering communication during disputes often leads to more constructive resolutions and lessens relationship distress *(Gottman, 1994)*. When couples communicate empathetically during disagreements, they are more likely to achieve mutually satisfying outcomes, fostering resilience and harmony within the relationship.

The development of trust and emotional intimacy between partners is significantly influenced by empowerment. Empirical evidence indicates that couples practicing empowerment are more likely to feel secure and emotionally bonded in their relationship *(Wieselquist, Rusbult, Foster, & Agnew, 1999)*. This enhanced emotional closeness, in turn, augments marital satisfaction and provides a safeguard against potential relationship dissolution.

Empowerment is integral to maintaining a balanced distribution of power within a marriage. Research reveals that couples promoting each other's autonomy and decision-making abilities tend to report higher satisfaction and superior relationship quality *(Sprecher, 2001)*. Couples can cultivate a balanced and supportive dynamic by nurturing empowerment within their partnership.

In addition to these aspects, empowerment significantly influences how couples navigate the inevitable life transitions in a marriage's lifespan. Studies suggest that couples who support each other's growth, needs, and aspirations during pivotal life transitions such as career changes, childbirth, or the challenges of aging, display a more remarkable ability to adapt and sustain their relationship satisfaction *(Birditt, Wan, Orbuch, & Antonucci, 2017)*. Empowerment provides couples the tools to support each other through these transitions, fostering a resilient and enduring partnership.

To illustrate, imagine a scenario where one partner embarks on a new career trajectory. The partner practicing empowerment can support the other's aspirations, encourage their development, and aid them in navigating the challenges associated with this shift. This empowering approach helps preserve the relationship's harmony and stability while fostering personal and professional growth.

Couples who emphasize empowerment in their interactions, conflict resolution, expressions of intimacy, and transitions will likely experience heightened marital satisfaction, stronger emotional bonds, and improved resilience when faced with challenges.

Explanation

Empowerment is an essential component of a healthy marriage. When we can support and encourage our partners in their goals and aspirations, we create a sense of mutual empowerment that allows our relationship to thrive. So, how do these biblical verses tie into the idea of empowerment in marriage?

Biblical Foundation

1 Thessalonians 5:11 (NIV) – "Therefore encourage one another and build each other up, just as in fact you are doing."

Hebrews 10:24 (NIV) – "And let us consider how we may spur one another on toward love and good deeds."

Let's start with 1 Thessalonians 5:11. This verse encourages us to encourage and build each other up. By being supportive and positive towards our partners, we create a sense of empowerment that allows them to confidently pursue their goals. When we're able to celebrate each other's accomplishments and support each other through challenges, we build a stronger and more fulfilling relationship.

In Hebrews 10:24, this verse reminds us to spur one another toward love and good deeds. By being an active source of support and encouragement for our partners, we can help them achieve their full potential and positively impact the world. When we can empower each other in this way, we create a sense of purpose and meaning in our marriage that can bring us closer together.

So, what do these verses mean for you as a couple who wants to cultivate empowerment in your marriage? They emphasize the importance of being supportive, positive, and encouraging toward each other. By practicing empowerment in your daily interactions, you can create a sense of mutual support and fulfillment that allows your marriage to thrive.

Summary

Empowerment, as essential to marriage as trust or love, emphasizes mutual support and growth. Academic research establishes a profound connection between empowerment and marital satisfaction. Couples that empower each other strengthen their emotional bond and equip themselves to face and overcome relationship challenges. Empowering each other also helps in effective conflict resolution, builds trust and emotional intimacy, and ensures a balanced power dynamic in marriage. Notably, during life's inevitable transitions, empowerment acts as the foundation upon which couples can rely, ensuring longevity and adaptability in the relationship.

The Bible champions the spirit of empowerment. Verses such as 1 Thessalonians 5:11 and Hebrews 10:24 remind couples of the importance of encouragement and mutual growth. They stress building each other up, supporting aspirations, and pushing each other towards love and benevolence. For couples aiming to imbue their relationship with empowerment, these teachings offer a blueprint: to consistently uplift, support, and motivate each other.

By integrating these principles into everyday interactions and being mindful of different religious and cultural perspectives, couples can lay the foundation for a profoundly supportive and thriving marriage.

Applying The Lesson: Empowerment Power Hour

Activity 1: Devotional Commencement – Empowerment (3 Minutes)
- Together, find a spot and offer a prayer of gratitude for exploring "Empowerment".

Activity 2: Purposeful Pondering (2 Minutes)
- Pause to set joint intentions and share aspirations for the session.

Activity 3: Insight Exchange (10 Minutes)
- Spend 10 minutes writing or reviewing "Empowerment" notes, then share summaries.

Activity 4: Scripture Insights (10 Minutes)
- Read 1 Thessalonians 5:11 and Hebrews 10:24 together, taking turns to share insights and personal applications. Now, each of you find a different bible verse that speaks to the topic. Discuss your choice and why.

Activity 5: Bonding over Devotion (20 Minutes)
Choose and immerse yourselves in ONE of the provided activity options, aiming to deepen understanding, enjoy the process, and fortify your connection.

- **OPTION A:** Power Praise – Each share a recent achievement, with the other providing positive feedback and praise. Discuss the emotional uplift.
- **OPTION B:** Empowerment Role Play – Act out a scenario where one empowers the other. Discuss the feelings invoked.

Activity 6: Constructive Feedback Circle (10 Minutes)
- Reflect on a time empowerment was challenging and discuss how it could have been better.

Activity 7: Gratitude Moment (2 Minutes)
- Share something you're each thankful for about the other.

Activity 8: Intimate Intercession (3 Minutes)
Spend a few minutes in silent meditation and prayer, focusing on each other, and conclude with a joint "Amen."

Lesson Notes and Summary for Sharing

REFLECTIONS

Lesson Notes:

Summary:

Weekly Journal Notes

(Complete before Next Session)

EMPOWERMENT NOTES AND JOURNAL

I WILL:

Continue to:

Stop:

E: Empowerment

| I WILL: |

Start:

Reflections:

CHAPTER 7

R: Resilience

Overcoming Obstacles Together: The Pillars Of Resilience In Marriage

Lesson Objective: To help you understand the importance of resilience in marriage and develop skills to persevere through difficult times while maintaining hope for the future.

An Academic Perspective

Resilience, the ability to recover from or adjust easily to adversity or change, is vital in successful marriages. Academic research in this field offers profound insights, suggesting resilience can serve as an anchor in sustaining marriages across various life stages.

Marital satisfaction significantly correlates to the degree of resilience demonstrated between partners. Studies highlight that resilience, which involves the capacity to weather difficulties and sustain optimism for the future, is positively linked with higher marital satisfaction *(Bradbury & Lavner, 2012)*. Couples who embody resilience are more adept at maintaining a robust emotional connection and tackling challenges, which results in a richer and more rewarding marital life.

Resilience is crucial to effective conflict resolution and critical to a marriage's stability and success. Research has found that resilient communication during conflicts often leads to constructive outcomes and reduced relationship distress *(Bodenmann, Meuwly, & Kayser, 2011)*. When couples communicate with resilience during disagreements, they're more inclined to reach mutually agreeable resolutions, cultivating harmony and longevity in the relationship.

Development of trust and emotional intimacy, fundamental aspects of a marriage, are significantly aided by resilience. Studies suggest that when confronted with adversity, resilient couples tend to feel more secure and emotionally attached to their relationship *(Holley et al., 2010)*. Such emotional bonding not only amplifies marital satisfaction but also acts as a deterrent against potential relationship breakdowns.

Resilience is critical to striking a healthy balance between individual aspirations and shared goals in marriage. Research demonstrates that couples who exhibit resilience by backing each other's personal ambitions while fostering shared objectives experience superior relationship satisfaction and overall quality of relationships *(Stanley, Markman, & Whitton, 2002)*. By nurturing resilience, couples can engender a supportive and balanced relationship dynamic.

The relevance of resilience is also manifested in how couples navigate life's inevitable changes that transpire in a marriage. Studies indicate that couples displaying resilience while supporting each other's development and aspirations during significant life events, such as career changes or the birth of a child, are better equipped to adapt and preserve their relationship satisfaction *(Karney & Bradbury, 1995)*. Resilience empowers couples to provide mutual support and traverse these changes, nurturing a lasting and adaptive partnership.

Consider, for instance, a scenario where a couple needs to relocate due to one partner's career opportunity. By practicing resilience, both partners can provide mutual support during the challenges and uncertainties of moving, acclimating to a new environment, and building a fresh social network. This resilient approach preserves the harmony and stability of the relationship while actively embracing collective growth and change.

Couples prioritizing resilience in their interactions, conflict resolution, intimate expressions, and approach to life transitions are likely to report higher marital satisfaction, stronger emotional bonds, and improved adaptability when faced with adversity. The cultivation of resilience in relationships, therefore, serves as the bedrock of a successful and rewarding marital journey for couples across various life stages.

Biblical Foundation

Romans 5:3-4 (NIV) – "Not only so, but we also glory in our sufferings, because we know that suffering produces perseverance; perseverance, character; and character, hope."

Ecclesiastes 4:12 (NIV) – "Though one may be overpowered, two can defend themselves. A cord of three strands is not quickly broken."

Explanation

Resilience is an important quality to cultivate in a healthy marriage. When we can weather the storms of life together and bounce back from adversity, we create a sense of mutual support and strength that allows our relationship to thrive. So, how do these biblical verses tie into the idea of resilience in marriage?

Let's start with Romans 5:3-4. This verse reminds us that suffering can actually produce perseverance, character, and hope. When we can face challenges together and overcome them, we build a sense of resilience and strength that can help us tackle any obstacle that comes our way. By working together and relying on our faith, we can turn even the most difficult situations into opportunities for growth and transformation.

In Ecclesiastes 4:12, this verse emphasizes the power of partnership and unity. When facing difficult times, we're not alone - we have our partner. By working together and supporting each other, we can create a bond of resilience that allows us to overcome any challenge. As the verse says, "A cord of three strands is not quickly broken." When we're united in purpose and committed to each other, we become stronger than we ever could be on our own.

So, what do these verses mean for you as a couple who wants to cultivate resilience in your marriage? They emphasize the importance of facing challenges together, relying on your faith, and supporting each other through difficult times. By practicing resilience in your daily interactions, you can create a sense of mutual support and strength that allows your marriage to thrive.

Summary

Resilience, the hallmark of bouncing back from adversity, is paramount for a flourishing marriage. Scholarly investigations highlight the importance of resilience in safeguarding marital satisfaction. Resilient couples are better equipped to navigate relationship challenges, ensuring emotional closeness even during tough times. They also excel in conflict resolution, creating a harmonious and lasting bond. Additionally, resilience enhances trust and emotional intimacy, two pillars of a thriving marriage. By promoting individual dreams and joint ventures, resilience fosters a balanced and supportive relationship dynamic. Moreover, as couples face life's transitions, resilience aids in mutual support, fostering adaptability and ensuring satisfaction in the relationship.

The Bible emphasizes resilience. Romans 5:3-4 illustrates how adversity can pave the way for perseverance, character, and hope. Together, couples can transform challenges into growth opportunities. Ecclesiastes 4:12 underscores the strength of the partnership, suggesting that unity amplifies resilience, making the marital bond unbreakable. These teachings provide guidance for couples aiming to instill resilience in their relationship: face challenges together, lean on faith, and offer unwavering support. By emphasizing resilience in daily interactions and being considerate of different religious and cultural perspectives, couples lay the groundwork for a dynamic, enduring marriage.

Applying The Lesson: Resilience Power Hour

Activity 1: Devotional Commencement – Resilience (3 Minutes)
- Together, find a spot and offer a prayer of gratitude for exploring "Resilience".

Activity 2: Purposeful Pondering (2 Minutes)
- Pause to set joint intentions and share aspirations for the session.

Activity 3: Insight Exchange (10 Minutes)
- Spend 10 minutes writing or reviewing "Resilience" notes, then share summaries.

Activity 4: Scripture Insights (10 Minutes)
- Read Romans 5:3-4 and Ecclesiastes 4:12 together, taking turns to share insights and personal applications. Now, each of you find a different bible verse that speaks to the topic. Discuss your choice and why.

Activity 5: Bonding over Devotion (20 Minutes)

Choose and immerse yourselves in ONE of the provided activity options, aiming to deepen understanding, enjoy the process, and fortify your connection.

- **OPTION A:** Resilience Recall – Narrate a past challenge you both overcame. Discuss the strengths harnessed.
- **OPTION B:** Barrier Break Chat – Talk about current obstacles and devise a joint strategy to overcome them.

Activity 6: Constructive Feedback Circle (10 Minutes)
- Reflect on a time resilience was challenging and discuss how it could have been better.

Activity 7: Gratitude Moment (2 Minutes)
- Share something you're each thankful for about the other.

Activity 8: Intimate Intercession (3 Minutes)

Spend a few minutes in silent meditation and prayer, focusing on each other, and conclude with a joint "Amen."

Lesson Notes and Summary for Sharing

REFLECTIONS

Lesson Notes:

Summary:

Weekly Journal Notes

(Complete before Next Session)

RESILIENCE NOTES AND JOURNAL

I WILL:

Continue to:

Stop:

R: Resilience

I WILL:

Start:

Reflections:

CHAPTER 8

W: Wellness

A Well-Balanced Life: Prioritizing Wellness For A Thriving Partnership

---

Lesson Objective: To help you understand the importance of wellness in marriage and develop skills to prioritize physical, emotional, and spiritual wellness.

An Academic Perspective

Wellness, which includes how we feel physically, emotionally, and spiritually, is crucial to keeping marriages strong and happy. Studies show that caring for ourselves in these ways is important for couples of all ages, helping them build lasting and meaningful relationships.

The level of well-being in partners significantly impacts how happy they are in their marriage. Research consistently shows a clear link between well-being –taking care of the body, emotions, and spirit – and a stronger marriage *(Hawkins & Fackrell, 2010)*. When couples consciously try to focus on their well-being, they can better maintain a strong emotional bond and handle problems in their relationship. This leads to a deeper and more fulfilling connection.

Wellness plays a vital role in many aspects of a successful marriage. It affects how couples resolve conflicts, build trust, achieve personal and shared goals, and navigate life changes together. Research consistently highlights the positive impact of wellness on various aspects of marital well-being.

When partners prioritize their physical, emotional, and spiritual well-being during disagreements, they tend to find better solutions and experience less stress *(Papp, Cummings, & Goeke-Morey, 2009)*. This approach enhances harmony and fosters emotional intimacy, making couples feel more connected and secure *(Karney & Bradbury, 1995)*.

Maintaining wellness helps couples balance their individual goals with shared aspirations. Supporting each other's well-being while pursuing common dreams increases relationship satisfaction and quality *(Sullivan, Pasch, Johnson, & Bradbury, 2010)*. This creates a supportive partnership where both individuals thrive.

Wellness is also crucial to managing the changes that come with time. Couples who focus on wellness can better navigate life transitions such as career shifts, parenthood, or aging, strengthening their relationship's resilience *(Donoho, Crimmins, & Seeman, 2013)*. By prioritizing wellness, couples support each other through these changes, fostering a lasting and adaptable bond.

Consider a couple becoming parents. Prioritizing wellness enables them to face the challenges of parenthood while maintaining their health and connection. This commitment helps them grow as individuals and partners while embracing new roles.

Couples that infuse wellness into their daily interactions, conflict resolutions, intimacy expressions, and responses to life's ups and downs report higher marital satisfaction, deeper emotional bonds, and increased ability to overcome challenges. Prioritizing wellness offers couples a blueprint for a fulfilling and enduring marriage.

Explanation

Wellness holds a crucial place within a flourishing marriage. When we tend to our physical, mental, and spiritual health, we establish a solid base to construct a resilient and enriching partnership with our partner. But how do these biblical passages align with the concept of wellness in marriage?

Let's begin with 3 John 1:2. This verse underlines that our health and well-being carry significance in the eyes of God.

Biblical Foundation

3 John 1:2 (NIV) – "Dear friend, I pray that you may enjoy good health and that all may go well with you, even as your soul is getting along well."

1 Corinthians 6:19-20 (NIV) – "Do you not know that your bodies are temples of the Holy Spirit, who is in you, whom you have received from God? You are not your own; you were bought at a price. Therefore honor God with your bodies."

When we nurture our physical and spiritual selves, we achieve harmony and completeness, empowering us to bring our best selves to our marriage. By placing importance on our well-being, we set in motion a positive influence that reaches every facet of our existence, including our connection with our partner.

Moving ahead to 1 Corinthians 6:19-20, this scripture reminds us that our bodies serve as temples of the Holy Spirit. This implies a duty to care for our bodies and honor their sanctity. When we prioritize our physical well-being through exercise, nourishment, and rest, we lay a foundation of wellness that allows us to flourish in all spheres, including our marital relationship.

So, what do these verses signify for you as a couple striving to foster wellness in your marriage? They underscore the significance of tending to your physical, mental, and spiritual dimensions to present your best selves within your partnership. By practicing self-care and regarding your bodies as vessels of reverence, you forge a robust wellness base that nurtures the thriving of your marriage.

Summary

Wellness, encompassing our physical, emotional, and spiritual health, is a cornerstone for nurturing robust and joyful marriages. Scholarly insights shed light on the intrinsic connection between a partner's well-being and marital happiness. Couples who cultivate wellness can sustain emotional connections, navigate relationship challenges, and build profound bonds. Such wellness influences conflict resolutions, personal and joint aspirations, and how couples deal with life's transitions. For instance, when partners embark on the journey of parenthood, prioritizing wellness aids in confronting new challenges, ensuring health, and maintaining their connection.

The Bible echoes the significance of wellness in marriage. 3 John 1:2 emphasizes that our physical and spiritual well-being is dear to God and is pivotal in leading a harmonious life. Through this harmony, couples can further amplify their marital bond. 1 Corinthians 6:19-20 reminds us of our bodies' sacredness, vessels of the Holy Spirit. This scripture underscores the duty to cherish and care for our bodies, reinforcing the foundation of wellness. This dedication to wellness enriches individual well-being and contributes positively to marital health.

A dual approach that combines academic understanding and biblical teachings can be instrumental for couples aiming to intertwine wellness within their marriage. Respecting various cultural and religious backgrounds while focusing on wellness forms the bedrock of a caring, resilient, and harmonious marital relationship.

Applying The Lesson: Wellness Power Hour

Activity 1: Devotional Commencement – Wellness (3 Minutes)
- Together, find a spot and offer a prayer of gratitude for exploring "Wellness".

Activity 2: Purposeful Pondering (2 Minutes)
- Pause to set joint intentions and share aspirations for the session.

Activity 3: Insight Exchange (10 Minutes)
- Spend 10 minutes writing or reviewing "Wellness" notes, then share summaries.

Activity 4: Scripture Insights (10 Minutes)
- Read 3 John 1:2 and 1 Corinthians 6:19-20 together, taking turns to share insights and personal applications. Now, each of you find a different bible verse that speaks to the topic. Discuss your choice and why.

Activity 5: Bonding over Devotion (20 Minutes)
Choose and immerse yourselves in ONE of the provided activity options, aiming to deepen understanding, enjoy the process, and fortify your connection.

- **OPTION A:** Wellness Wheel – Discuss a wellness activity you'd like to pursue together, from diet to mental health.
- **OPTION B:** Quick Wellness Activity – Engage in a short, mutual wellness activity like deep breathing, and share the experience.

Activity 6: Constructive Feedback Circle (10 Minutes)
- Reflect on a time wellness was challenging and discuss how it could have been better.

Activity 7: Gratitude Moment (2 Minutes)
- Share something you're each thankful for about the other.

Activity 8: Intimate Intercession (3 Minutes)
Spend a few minutes in silent meditation and prayer, focusing on each other, and conclude with a joint "Amen."

Lesson Notes and Summary for Sharing

REFLECTIONS

Lesson Notes:

Summary:

Weekly Journal Notes

(Complete before Next Session)

WELLNESS NOTES AND JOURNAL

I WILL:

Continue to:

Stop:

W: Wellness

I WILL:

Start:

Reflections:

CHAPTER 9

E: Emotional Intelligence

Emotional Wisdom:
Strengthening Your Marriage Through Emotional Intelligence

Lesson Objective: To help you understand the importance of emotional intelligence in marriage and develop skills to understand, manage, and respond to emotions in oneself and others.

An Academic Perspective

Emotional intelligence, which involves recognizing, understanding, handling, and utilizing emotions effectively, is crucial in marital bonds. Extensive academic research illustrates the significance of emotional intelligence in marriages, offering insights valuable to couples of different life stages.

Studies consistently link emotional intelligence to marital contentment. The ability to comprehend, manage, and react adeptly to emotions in oneself and one's partner is associated with higher levels of marital satisfaction *(Brackett et al., 2005)*. Couples with vital emotional intelligence often excel at maintaining emotional closeness and navigating challenges, leading to more rewarding relationships.

Emotional intelligence is pivotal in conflict resolution and vital for a solid and fruitful marriage. Research demonstrates that emotionally intelligent communication during conflicts produces more productive resolutions and decreases relationship strain *(Schutte et al., 2001)*. When couples apply emotional intelligence during disagreements, they are more likely to find solutions that satisfy both parties, fostering harmony and resilience.

Emotional intelligence also fosters trust and emotional intimacy between partners. Evidence suggests that couples adept in emotional intelligence, especially during difficult times, tend to feel secure and emotionally connected *(Zeidner et al., 2012)*. This emotional bond enhances marital satisfaction and safeguards against relationship breakdown.

Additionally, emotional intelligence is essential for balancing personal and shared goals in marriage. Research reveals that couples practicing emotional intelligence – addressing each other's emotional needs while nurturing common aspirations – experience greater relationship contentment and higher overall quality *(Malouff et al., 2014)*. Couples create a supportive and balanced relationship dynamic by nurturing emotional intelligence in their partnership.

Emotional intelligence also guides couples through the inevitable changes that accompany marriage. Studies show that couples skilled in emotional intelligence – supporting each other during significant life shifts like career changes, having children, or facing aging – adapt better and maintain satisfaction *(Kotov et al., 2017)*. Emotional intelligence empowers couples to provide mutual support and face these changes, fostering resilience.

Imagine a couple dealing with a significant financial setback. By applying emotional intelligence, the couple comprehends each other's emotions, manages their feelings effectively, and offers supportive responses. This approach preserves the harmony of their relationship while confronting the challenge unitedly.

Couples incorporating emotional intelligence into their interactions, conflict resolutions, intimacy, and approach to changes often report greater marital satisfaction, intensified emotional connections, and enhanced resilience. Hence, nurturing emotional intelligence within a relationship provides couples of all ages a foundation for a successful and fulfilling marriage.

Biblical Foundation

Proverbs 15:1 (NIV) – "A gentle answer turns away wrath, but a harsh word stirs up anger."

Explanation

Galatians 5:22-23 (NIV) – "But the fruit of the Spirit is love, joy, peace, forbearance, kindness, goodness, faithfulness, gentleness and self-control. Against such things there is no law."

Emotional intelligence stands as a vital pillar in a thriving marriage. When we can comprehend and manage our emotions, along with being attuned to our partner's feelings, we foster an environment of mutual understanding and respect that nurtures our relationship. But how do these biblical verses align with the concept of emotional intelligence in marriage?

Let's begin with Proverbs 15:1. This verse highlights that responding with gentleness can defuse anger, while harsh words can escalate tensions. When we communicate with our partner gently and respectfully, we establish a secure and nurturing space that propels our relationship to flourish. By practicing emotional intelligence in communication, we can sidestep needless conflicts and construct a more robust and enriching marriage.

Moving forward to Galatians 5:22-23, this verse outlines the virtues of the Spirit, encompassing love, joy, peace, patience, kindness, goodness, faithfulness, gentleness, and self-control. By nurturing these qualities in our lives and our connection with our partner, we foster emotional intelligence that equips us to navigate life's ebb and flow with poise and resilience. Through daily interactions infused with emotional intelligence, we cultivate a more profound understanding, mutual respect, and thriving marriage.

So, what do these verses signify for you as a couple aspiring to cultivate emotional intelligence in your marriage? They underscore the significance of comprehending and managing your emotions while attuning to your partner's feelings. Integrating emotional intelligence into your communication and interactions lays the foundation for a robust and fulfilling marriage founded on mutual understanding and respect.

Summary

Emotional intelligence is vital for strong marriages. Recognizing, understanding, and managing emotions can lead to greater marital satisfaction. Research shows that couples who value emotional intelligence have deeper connections, handle conflicts more effectively, and create lasting bonds.

From the Bible, Proverbs 15:1 teaches the importance of gentle communication, reinforcing that understanding and kindness can prevent and resolve conflicts. On the other hand, Galatians 5:22-23 highlights virtues like love, patience, and kindness, which are essential components of emotional intelligence. By embracing these values, couples can build a relationship based on mutual respect and understanding.

In short, blending emotional intelligence with lessons from the Bible can help couples foster a loving and supportive marriage, appreciating differences and celebrating common ground.

Applying The Lesson: Emotional Intelligence Power Hour

Activity 1: Devotional Commencement – Emotional Intelligence (3 Minutes)
- Together, find a spot and offer a prayer of gratitude for exploring "Emotional Intelligence".

Activity 2: Purposeful Pondering (2 Minutes)
- Pause to set joint intentions and share aspirations for the session.

Activity 3: Insight Exchange (10 Minutes)
- Spend 10 minutes writing or reviewing "Emotional Intelligence" notes, then share summaries.

Activity 4: Scripture Insights (10 Minutes)
- Read Proverbs 15:1 and Galatians 5:22-23 together, taking turns to share insights and personal applications. Now, each of you find a different bible verse that speaks to the topic. Discuss your choice and why.

Activity 5: Bonding over Devotion (20 Minutes)
Choose and immerse yourselves in ONE of the provided activity options, aiming to deepen understanding, enjoy the process, and fortify your connection.

- **OPTION A:** Emotion Imitation Game – Imitate an emotion without words, letting the other guess. Discuss the accuracy and depth of understanding.
- **OPTION B:** E.I. Chat – Talk about a recent event where emotional intelligence played a role and share insights.

Activity 6: Constructive Feedback Circle (10 Minutes)
- Reflect on a time emotional intelligence was challenging and discuss how it could have been better.

Activity 7: Gratitude Moment (2 Minutes)
- Share something you're each thankful for about the other.

Activity 8: Intimate Intercession (3 Minutes)
Spend a few minutes in silent meditation and prayer, focusing on each other, and conclude with a joint "Amen."

Lesson Notes and Summary for Sharing

REFLECTIONS

Lesson Notes:

Summary:

Weekly Journal Notes

(Complete before Next Session)

EMOTIONAL INTELLIGENCE NOTES AND JOURNAL

I WILL:

Continue to:

Stop:

I WILL:

Start:

Reflections:

CHAPTER 10

D: Devotion

A Lifelong Commitment: The Beauty Of Devotion In Marriage

Lesson Objective: To help you understand the importance of devotion in marriage and develop skills to foster commitment, loyalty, and unwavering love for one's partner.

An Academic Perspective

*I*n marriages, devotion is pivotal in nurturing successful and enduring unions. Devotion encompasses commitment, loyalty, and unwavering love, and researchers have extensively examined its significance. The insights gained are pertinent to couples in various life stages.

Rusbult et al.'s study in 1998 highlighted that the level of devotion shared between partners deeply affects marital satisfaction. This form of devotion, characterized by commitment, steadfast affection, and unwavering loyalty, correlates with heightened marital contentment. Demonstrating such devotion empowers couples to maintain strong emotional bonds and adeptly navigate relationship challenges. This ability leads to a more satisfying relationship and one that fulfills multiple dimensions.

Conflict resolution, a vital component of thriving marriages, is also intricately linked to devotion. Fincham et al.'s research in 2007 observed that devoted couples approach conflicts with patience, understanding, and a willingness to compromise. This constructive conflict approach often results in positive outcomes, reduces relationship strain, and fosters harmony and resilience in the marriage.

Trust and emotional intimacy, foundational elements of strong relationships, are significantly influenced by devotion. According to Le et al.'s study in 2010, couples exhibiting high levels of devotion tend to experience a profound sense of security and emotional closeness. This emotional intimacy not only enhances marital satisfaction but also acts as a potent shield against potential relationship dissolution, contributing to the longevity of the marital bond.

Devotion also plays a pivotal role in striking a delicate balance between personal and shared aspirations within marriage. Stanley et al.'s research in 2010 demonstrated that couples practicing devotion by supporting each other's individual needs while nurturing joint goals reported greater relationship contentment. Such devotion fosters a supportive and harmonious relationship dynamic, enhancing overall relationship quality.

Navigating life's transitions is an inherent aspect of marriage. The role of devotion in managing these transitions is paramount. Rhoades et al.'s study in 2012 revealed that couples displaying devotion by offering support during significant life changes, such as career shifts or the arrival of a child, were better equipped to adapt and sustain relationship satisfaction.

For instance, envision a couple grappling with a serious health challenge. Through devotion, they provide unwavering support and encouragement to one another during this difficult time. Such devotion preserves the stability of their relationship while they confront and surmount the challenge together.

Explanation

Devotion emerges as a cornerstone of a flourishing and meaningful marriage. When we prioritize our bond with our partner and showcase our love and unwavering commitment, we foster an environment of shared respect and gratitude that nurtures the growth of our relationship. But how do these biblical verses align with the concept of devotion in marriage?

Biblical Foundation

Ephesians 5:25 (NIV) – "Husbands, love your wives, just as Christ loved the church and gave himself up for her."

Proverbs 31:10-12 (NIV) – "A wife of noble character who can find? She is worth far more than rubies. Her husband has full confidence in her and lacks nothing of value. She brings him good, not harm, all the days of her life."

Let's begin with Ephesians 5:25. This verse underscores the significance of husbands loving their spouses like Christ loved the church. This love is marked by sacrifice, putting the needs and welfare of the partner ahead of one's own. By demonstrating this selfless love and devotion, husbands lay the groundwork for a relationship built on trust and mutual respect, allowing their marriage to thrive.

Shifting to Proverbs 31:10-12, this verse characterizes a wife of noble character as invaluable. It highlights the importance of a wife who is reliable, esteemed, and dedicated to her husband. By bringing goodness and fostering an environment of respect, she contributes to the thriving of their relationship. This dedication and commitment are keystones in constructing a robust and fulfilling marriage.

So, what do these verses signify for you as a couple aspiring to nurture devotion in your marriage? They underline the necessity of placing your relationship at the forefront and showcasing your love and unwavering commitment. By infusing devotion into your daily interactions, you pave the way for trust and respect to flourish, serving as the bedrock on which your marriage thrives.

During this journey, you've encountered activities and exercises tailored to help you cultivate devotion within your marriage. Engaging in these activities together deepen your comprehension of one another and fortify your connection as a couple.

Summary

Devotion in marriage stands as a core pillar, enveloping unwavering commitment, steadfast loyalty, and deep-seated love. Scientific research illustrates how devotion directly correlates with aspects of marital life, including satisfaction, conflict resolution, trust-building, and the ability to adeptly navigate life's inevitable transitions.

Ephesians 5:25 eloquently encapsulates the essence of devotion. It challenges husbands to love their wives with a depth and selflessness parallel to Christ's love for the church, signifying a love willing to prioritize the partner's well-being. In contrast, Proverbs 31:10-12 highlights the invaluable character of a devoted wife, emphasizing her dedication and the positive impact of her unwavering commitment to the marital bond.

These biblical passages serve as guiding beacons for couples, encouraging them to anchor their relationship in a profound sense of devotion. By intertwining this dedication with the insights from academic studies, couples can sculpt a resilient, fulfilling marital bond that is deeply rooted in mutual respect and understanding. Embracing devotion holistically offers couples a fortified foundation, ensuring their marriage remains strong amidst life's ebb and flow.

Applying The Lesson: Devotion Power Hour

Activity 1: Devotional Commencement – Devotion (3 Minutes)
- Together, find a spot and offer a prayer of gratitude for exploring "Devotion".

Activity 2: Purposeful Pondering (2 Minutes)
- Pause to set joint intentions and share aspirations for the session.

Activity 3: Insight Exchange (10 Minutes)
- Spend 10 minutes writing or reviewing "Devotion" notes, then share summaries.

Activity 4: Scripture Insights (10 Minutes)
- Read Ephesians 5:25 and Proverbs 31:10-12 together, taking turns to share insights and personal applications. Now, each of you find a different bible verse that speaks to the topic. Discuss your choice and why.

Activity 5: Bonding over Devotion (20 Minutes)
Choose and immerse yourselves in ONE of the provided activity options, aiming to deepen understanding, enjoy the process, and fortify your connection.

- **OPTION A:** Devotion Diary – Each partner briefly writes a note about a time the other displayed devotion. Swap and discuss.
- **OPTION B:** Devotion Discussion – Talk about acts of devotion you value most and express appreciation.

Activity 6: Constructive Feedback Circle (10 Minutes)
- Reflect on a time devotion was challenging and discuss how it could have been better.

Activity 7: Gratitude Moment (2 Minutes)
- Share something you're each thankful for about the other.

Activity 8: Intimate Intercession (3 Minutes)
Spend a few minutes in silent meditation and prayer, focusing on each other, and conclude with a joint "Amen."

Lesson Notes and Summary for Sharing

REFLECTIONS

Lesson Notes:

Summary:

Weekly Journal Notes

(Complete before Next Session)

DEVOTION NOTES AND JOURNAL

I WILL:

Continue to:

Stop:

D: Devotion

I WILL:

Start:

Reflections:

Final Reflections on F.O.R.E.V.E.R. W.E.D.

Thank you for engaging with the *F.O.R.E.V.E.R. W.E.D.* Workbook for Couples. You've delved into vital relationship cornerstones: Flexibility, Open Communication, Respect, Empathy, Vulnerability, Empowerment, Resilience, Wellness, Emotional Intelligence, and Devotion. These aren't just concepts but pillars for a harmonious, enduring union.

As you step forward in your shared journey, remember to embody the essence of *F.O.R.E.V.E.R. W.E.D.* daily. Here are actionable strategies to assist you:

- **Consistent Check-ins:** Designate weekly times for open dialogue. This encourages transparency and strengthens your bond.
- **Empathetic Listening:** Listen to understand. Resist making assumptions, and always prioritize clarity.
- **Express Gratitude:** Regularly affirm and appreciate each other. Such gestures solidify mutual respect.
- **Self-Care Focus:** Prioritize individual well-being. Embrace activities that uplift, and champion your partner's well-being pursuits.

- **Seek Support:** When challenges arise, embrace resilience by turning to trusted individuals or professionals. Remember, it's a sign of strength.

Let these practices be the threads that weave the *F.O.R.E.V.E.R. W.E.D.* principles into the fabric of your marriage.

Wishing you a future where your shared dedication continues to bloom, lighting the path for many beautiful tomorrows.

Warm Regards,
Dr. Cedric Alford

References

Allen, E. S., Atkins, D. C., Baucom, D. H., Snyder, D. K., Gordon, K. C., & Glass, S. P. (2005). Intrapersonal, interpersonal, and contextual factors in engaging in and responding to extramarital involvement. Clinical Psychology: Science and Practice, 12(2), 101-130.

Atkins, D. C., Baucom, D. H., & Jacobson, N. S. (2001). Understanding infidelity: Correlates in a national random sample. Journal of Family Psychology, 15(4), 735.

Birditt, K. S., Wan, W. H., Orbuch, T. L., & Antonucci, T. C. (2017). The development of marital tension: Implications for divorce among married couples. Developmental Psychology, 53(10), 1995–2006. doi: 10.1037/dev0000369

Bodenmann, G., Ledermann, T., & Bradbury, T. N. (2007). Stress, sex, and satisfaction in marriage. Personal Relationships, 14(4), 551–569.

Bodenmann, G., Meuwly, N., & Kayser, K. (2011). Two conceptualizations of dyadic coping and their potential for predicting relationship quality and individual well-being. European Psychologist, 16(4), 255-266.

Brackett, M. A., Warner, R. M., & Bosco, J. S. (2005). Emotional intelligence and relationship quality among couples. Personal Relationships, 12(2), 197-212.

Bradbury, T. N., & Lavner, J. A. (2012). How can we improve preventive and educational interventions for intimate relationships? Behavior Therapy, 43(1), 113-122.

Byers, E. S. (2005). Relationship satisfaction and sexual satisfaction: A longitudinal study of individuals in long-term relationships. Journal of Sex Research, 42(2), 113-118.

Cramer, D. (2004). Emotional support, conflict, depression, and relationship satisfaction in a romantic partner. The Journal of Psychology, 138(6), 532-542.

Donoho, C. J., Crimmins, E. M., & Seeman, T. E. (2013). Marital quality, gender, and markers of inflammation in the MIDUS cohort. Journal of Marriage and Family, 75(1), 127-141.

Evans, J. St. B. T., & Stanovich, K. E. (2013). Dual-process theories of higher cognition advancing the debate. Perspectives on Psychological Science, 8(3), 223–241. https://doi.org/10.1177/1745691612460685

Falconier, M. K., Jackson, J. B., Hilpert, P., & Bodenmann, G. (2015). Dyadic coping and relationship satisfaction: A meta-analysis. Clinical Psychology Review, 42, 28–46.

Fincham, F. D., Stanley, S. M., & Beach, S. R. H. (2007). Transformative processes in marriage: An analysis of emerging trends. Journal of Marriage and Family, 69(2), 275-292.

Finkel, E. J., Eastwick, P. W., & Reis, H. T. (2015). Best research practices in psychology: Illustrating epistemological and pragmatic considerations with the case of relationship science. Journal of Personality and Social Psychology, 108(2), 275–297. https://doi.org/10.1037/pspi0000007

Fiske, S. T., & Taylor, S. E. (2013). Social cognition: From brains to culture. Sage.

Gawronski, B. (2004). Theory-based bias correction in dispositional inference: The fundamental attribution error is dead, long live the correspondence bias. European Review of Social Psychology, 15(1), 183-217. https://doi.org/10.1080/10463280440000026

Gordon, K. C., Baucom, D. H., & Snyder, D. K. (2004). An integrative intervention for promoting recovery from extramarital affairs. Journal of Marital and Family Therapy, 30(2), 213-231.

Gottman, J. M. (1994). What predicts divorce?: The relationship between marital processes and marital outcomes. Hillsdale, NJ: Lawrence Erlbaum Associates.

Gottman, J. M., & Levenson, R. W. (2000). The timing of divorce: Predicting when a couple will divorce over a 14-year period. Journal of Marriage and Family, 62(3), 737-745.

Gottman, J. M., & Levenson, R. W. (1992). Marital processes predictive of later dissolution: behavior, physiology, and health. Journal of Personality and Social Psychology, 63(2), 221.

Hahlweg, K., Kaiser, A., Christensen, A., Fehm-Wolfsdorf, G., & Groth, T. (2000). Self-report and observational assessment of couples' conflict: The concordance between the Communication Patterns Questionnaire and the KPI Observation System. Journal of Marriage and the Family, 62, 61–67. doi: 10.1111/j.1741-3737.2000.00061.x

Hawkins, A. J., & Fackrell, T. A. (2010). Does relationship and marriage education for lower-income couples work? A meta-analytic study of emerging research. Journal of Couple & Relationship Therapy, 9(2), 181-191.

Heavey, C. L., Layne, C., & Christensen, A. (1993). Gender and conflict structure in marital interaction: A replication and extension. Journal of Consulting and Clinical Psychology, 61(1), 16–27. doi: 10.1037/0022-006X.61.1.16

Heiman, J. R., Long, J. S., Smith, S. N., Fisher, W. A., Sand, M. S., & Rosen, R. C. (2011). Sexual satisfaction and relationship happiness in midlife and older couples in five countries. Archives of Sexual Behavior, 40(4), 741–753.

Hendrick, S. S. (1988). A generic measure of relationship satisfaction. Journal of Marriage and the Family, 50, 93-98. http://dx.doi.org/10.2307/352430

Holley, S. R., Haase, C. M., & Levenson, R. W. (2013). Age-related changes in demand–withdraw communication behaviors. Journal of Marriage and Family, 75(4), 822-836.

Karney, B. R., & Bradbury, T. N. (1995). The longitudinal course of marital quality and stability: A review of theory, methods, and research. Psychological Bulletin, 118(1), 3-34.

Kornrich, S., Brines, J., & Leupp, K. (2013). Egalitarianism, Housework, and Sexual Frequency in Marriage. American Sociological Review, 78(1), 26-50. doi: 10.1177/0003122412472340

Kotov, R. I., Gamez, W., Schmidt, F., & Watson, D. (2017). Linking "big" personality traits to anxiety, depressive, and substance use disorders: a meta-analysis. Psychological bulletin, 143(9), 950.

Langer, S. L., Brown, J. D., & Syrjala, K. L. (2009). Intrapersonal and interpersonal consequences of protective buffering among cancer patients and caregivers. Cancer, 115(S18), 4311-4325. doi:10.1002/cncr.24586.

Laurenceau, J., Barrett, L. F., & Pietromonaco, P. R. (1998). Intimacy as an interpersonal process: The importance of self-disclosure, partner disclosure, and perceived partner responsiveness in interpersonal exchanges. Journal of Personality and Social Psychology, 74(5), 1238–1251. doi: 10.1037/0022-3514.74.5.1238

Le, B., Dove, N. L., Agnew, C. R., Korn, M. S., & Mutso, A. A. (2010). Predicting nonmarital romantic relationship dissolution: A meta-analytic synthesis. Personal Relationships, 17(3), 377-390.

Long, E. C., Angera, J. J., Carter, S. J., Nakamoto, M., & Kalso, M. (1999). Understanding the one you love: A longitudinal assessment of an empathy training program for couples in romantic relationships. Family Relations, 285-293.

MacNeil, S., & Byers, E. S. (2005). Dyadic assessment of sexual self-disclosure and sexual satisfaction in heterosexual dating couples. Journal of Social and Personal Relationships, 22(2), 169–181. doi: 10.1177/0265407505050942

Malouff, J. M., Schutte, N. S., & Thorsteinsson, E. B. (2014). Trait emotional intelligence and romantic relationship satisfaction: A meta-analysis. The American Journal of Family Therapy, 42(1), 53-66.

Mark, K. P., Janssen, E., & Milhausen, R. R. (2011). Infidelity in heterosexual couples: demographic, interpersonal, and personality-related predictors of extradyadic sex. Archives of Sexual Behavior, 40(5), 971-982.

Markman, H. J., & Rhoades, G. K. (2012). Relationship education research: Current status and future directions. Journal of Marital and Family Therapy, 38(1), 169–200.

McNulty, J. K., Olson, M. A., Meltzer, A. L., & Shaffer, M. J. (2013). Though they may be unaware, newlyweds implicitly know whether their marriage will be satisfying. Science, 342(6162), 1119-1120. https://doi.org/10.1126/science.1243140

Mikulincer, M., & Shaver, P. R. (2007). Attachment in adulthood: Structure, dynamics, and change. New York, NY, US: Guilford Press.

Papp, L. M., Cummings, E. M., & Goeke-Morey, M. C. (2009). For richer, for poorer: Money as a topic of marital conflict in the home. Family Relations, 58(1), 91-103.

Pietromonaco, P. R., Uchino, B., & Dunkel Schetter, C. (2013). Close relationship processes and health: Implications of attachment theory for health and disease. Health Psychology, 32(5), 499.

Pulerwitz, J., Amaro, H., De Jong, W., Gortmaker, S. L., & Rudd, R. (2002). Relationship power, condom use and HIV risk among women in the USA. AIDS Care, 14(6), 789–800. doi: 10.1080/0954012021000031868

Randall, A. K., & Bodenmann, G. (2009). The role of stress on close relationships and marital satisfaction. Clinical psychology review, 29(2), 105-115. doi: 10.1016/j.cpr.2008.10.004

Rehman, U. S., Rellini, A. H., & Fallis, E. (2011). The importance of sexual self-disclosure to sexual satisfaction and functioning in committed relationships. Journal of Sexual Medicine, 8(11), 3108-3115. doi: 10.1111/j.1743-6109.2011.02439.x

Reis, H. T., & Shaver, P. R. (1988). Intimacy as an interpersonal process. In S. Duck (Ed.), Handbook of personal relationships: Theory, research and interventions (pp. 367-389). Chichester, England: Wiley.

Rhoades, G. K., Stanley, S. M., & Markman, H. J. (2012). The impact of the transition to cohabitation on relationship functioning: Cross-sectional and longitudinal findings. Journal of Family Psychology, 26(3), 348-358.Kornrich, S., Brines, J., & Leupp, K. (2013). Egalitarianism, Housework, and Sexual Frequency in Marriage. American Sociological Review, 78(1), 26-50. doi: 10.1177/0003122412472340

Rusbult, C. E., & Van Lange, P. A. M. (2003). Interdependence, interaction, and relationships. Annual Review of Psychology, 54, 351–375. doi: 10.1146/annurev.psych.54.101601.145059

Rusbult, C. E., Martz, J. M., & Agnew, C. R. (1998). The Investment Model Scale: Measuring commitment level, satisfaction level, quality of alternatives, and investment size. Personal Relationships, 5(4), 357-387.

Schutte, N. S., Malouff, J. M., Bobik, C., Coston, T. D., Greeson, C., Jedlicka, C., .. & Wendorf, G. (2001). Emotional intelligence and interpersonal relations. The Journal of social psychology, 141(4), 523-536.

Segrin, C., Hanzal, A., Donnerstein, C., Taylor, M., & Domschke, T. J. (2007). Social skills, psychological well-being, and the mediating role of perceived stress. Anxiety, Stress & Coping, 20(3), 321-329.

Siffert, A., & Schwarz, N. (2011). The role of vulnerability in conflict resolution. Journal of Conflict Resolution, 55(6), 919-941. doi: 10.1177/0022002711407584

South, S. C., Krueger, R. F., & Iacono, W. G. (2011). Understanding General and Specific Connections between Psychopathology and Marital Distress: A Model Based Approach. Journal of Abnormal Psychology, 120(4), 935–947. doi: 10.1037/a0025429

Sprecher, S. (2001). Equity and social exchange in dating couples: Associations with satisfaction, commitment, and stability. Journal of Marriage and Family, 63(3), 599–613. doi: 10.1111/j.1741-3737.2001.00599.x

Stanley, S. M., Markman, H. J., & Whitton, S. W. (2002). Communication, conflict, and commitment: Insights on the foundations of relationship success from a national survey. Family Process, 41(4), 659-675.

Stanley, S. M., Rhoades, G. K., & Whitton, S. W. (2010). Commitment: Functions, formation, and the securing of romantic attachment. Journal of Family Theory & Review, 2(4), 243-257.

Sullivan, K. T., Pasch, L. A., Johnson, M. D., & Bradbury, T. N. (2010). Social support, problem solving, and the longitudinal course of newlywed marriage. Journal of Personality and Social Psychology, 98(4), 631-644.

Weger Jr, H., Castle, G. R., & Emmett, M. C. (2010). Active Listening in Peer Interviews: The Influence of Message Paraphrasing on Perceptions of Listening Skill. International Journal of Listening, 24(1), 34-49. doi: 10.1080/10904010903466311

Wieselquist, J., Rusbult, C. E., Foster, C. A., & Agnew, C. R. (1999). Commitment, pro-relationship behavior, and trust in close relationships. Journal of Personality and Social Psychology, 77(5), 942–966. doi: 10.1037/0022-3514.77.5.942

Zeidner, M., Matthews, G., & Roberts, R. D. (2012). The emotional intelligence, health, and well-being nexus: What have we learned and what have we missed?. Applied Psychology: Health and Well-Being, 4(1), 1-30.

About the Author

DR. CEDRIC ALFORD'S journey weaves through the practicalities of the corporate sector, the dedication of academia, and the heartfelt mission of the non-profit world. This diverse path has equipped him to deeply understand human interactions and relationships in varied contexts.

However, when it comes to insights about marriage, his compass points firmly to home. Dr. Alford's most profound lessons and cherished memories come from over 25 years by the side of his wife, Bonita. Together, they have navigated the complexities of life, transforming challenges into opportunities for growth and deepening their connection in the process.

While Dr. Alford does not claim the title of a marriage therapist or psychologist, he shares from the heart, drawing on genuine, lived experiences. He believes in the power of authentic storytelling, not just as a means to teach but to connect, resonate, and inspire.

This workbook is a tribute to those stories, the journey he's embarked on with Bonita, and the shared experiences of couples everywhere. Dr. Alford's hope is that, in sharing his reflections and insights, he can offer you tools and perspectives to enrich your own relationship journey.

Having journeyed through this workbook, may you carry forward the shared wisdom, drawing from it to enrich your love, commitment, and growth narrative. Let this be a cherished chapter in your ongoing adventure together as every story unfolds.

www.ingramcontent.com/pod-product-compliance
Lightning Source LLC
Chambersburg PA
CBHW081159020426
42333CB00020B/2559